Investing in Shares for Beginners
Unlock the Power of Passive Income
by Jackson Kruger

ISBN: 978-1-9164629-2-2

Published by Rising Tide Press

Rising Tide Press Limited,

71 – 75 Shelton Street,

Covent Garden,

London,

WC2H 9JQ

www.RisingTidePress.co.uk

Requests to publish work from this book should be sent to:

enquiries@RisingTidePress.co.uk

Cover created by Sophie Lees Design

sophie.lees-design@outlook.com

Table of Contents

Disclaimer

This book is intended as a starting point and foundational text to springboard the reader into making rational and considered investment decisions. **I am not an accredited financial adviser or investment professional, and do not provide personalised investment advice.** Any content presented here, such as predictions, opinions, commentaries, forecasts, stock picks or suggestions, expressed or implied herein, is included solely for the purposes of information, education or entertainment. It should not be regarded as investment advice under any circumstances. **You are responsible for your own investment decisions and I will not be held liable for any actions you take as a consequence of reading this book.** Conduct your own due diligence and consult a licensed financial professional before committing to any investment decision. **All investments or trades carried out after reading this book are done so at your own risk.**

At the time of writing, all information was believed to be reliable, but its accuracy or completeness cannot be guaranteed. I will not be held responsible for any loss or damages, monetary or otherwise, resulting from investment decisions based on the aforementioned information, or anything else herein. Past results are not indicative of future performance. My objectives with this book are to educate and facilitate rational investment decisions, **conducted at your own discretion**.

I hope you enjoy the book and wish you every success in your financial endeavours!

Introduction

For most of my life, I had no idea about the mechanisms of investing and believed that stock markets were the exclusive playgrounds of wealthy individuals and gargantuan institutions. These naive notions were shattered just a few short years ago - almost by accident, in fact - when I stumbled across some articles and books about building wealth and achieving financial success. Much of this information was difficult to comprehend at first and took a substantial amount of study to get to grips with. Indeed, a certain degree of mysticism shrouds the financial markets, not to mention confusing terminology. It was like learning a new language at times! Therefore, it's not surprising that people find the markets so inaccessible that they leave everything to the so-called 'professionals'. Since biting the bullet and purchasing my first stock four years ago, I've discovered a great deal and have had steady and consistent investment returns.

In the beginning, I made some rather stupid mistakes, and will almost certainly make more on the journey towards my financial and career goals. My investing mindset is underpinned by **critical reflection on these errors**, accountability for them, and a constant desire for development and knowledge. I hope to pass on some of these concepts to you in this book. As you'll see in these pages, participation in the stock market can be tremendously powerful and life-changing but is **not without its risks**. Although these investment risks need to be acknowledged and respected accordingly, I would suggest that the proposition of having to work well into your twilight years because you can't afford to retire is **perhaps the riskiest scenario of all**. Sadly, this is the unfortunate reality for a growing number of people, a fact I regard as *a complete travesty*. This book is my small contribution to help address the 'knowledge gap' and make the process of investing a bit more accessible for the lay person.

Unfortunately, the concepts I'm about to share with you are not taught in schools, at least none that my family or I have ever attended. Therein lies my major motivation (or is it *aggravation?*) for writing this book. A certain degree of righteous indignation fuels my words, but also a sense of great hope and optimism. For a large chunk of society, the stock market is merely a barometer of the nation's economic and financial health. Most folks have no stake in its success or failure, and don't know all that much about it. Worse still, many are ignorant of what the stock market represents or have disastrous and costly misconceptions about it. I intend to critique a number of these perspectives in the following pages, before delving into my core investing ideas.

When I first started talking to work colleagues and family members about my newfound investing principles, it became apparent just how little many of them knew about the markets and how they can be used to **generate considerable wealth over the long term**. Many expressed feelings of concern and anxiety about the 'risks' involved and were scared that I would 'lose all my money'. This is perfectly understandable, as the Great Recession of 2007 - 2009 was, and still is, fresh in the public consciousness. Therefore, I think there is a dire need for accessible information on the topic, **the kind I wish I had in the very beginning**, to help people quell their fears and take the first steps in the direction of financial freedom. My objectives here are to convey the basic principles of **investing in shares for passive income streams** - money that comes to you for *doing nothing* - in a logical, concise and intuitive way. You too will be able to reap the benefits by taking personal responsibility for your financial future through making considered and rational investment decisions.

Why should you take my advice on board? I'm not wealthy or financially free (yet), and I certainly don't have any qualifications in financial planning or economics. My knowledge has been gleaned from reading widely, studying highly successful investors, analysing the principles they use to achieve success, and putting them into practice myself. Several key texts will be referenced throughout this book, and these are *highly recommended* if you want to develop your expertise and knowledge further. The goals of this book are to communicate often difficult investing concepts to the lay person. My credibility is grounded in my status as a regular individual, employed in higher education as a research student, with no financial affiliations of any kind. Perhaps most importantly, I have a genuine will to help people work towards monetary success, to empower their prosperity and live life on their own terms.

I hope this book helps you achieve all these goals and more! Good luck!

PART I
The Rational Basis for Income Investing

My Journey: Better Late than Never!

Early Education and Schooling

Like almost all kids that leave the state school production line in the United Kingdom, or most countries for that matter, I had little to no financial education. It was 2006, and I was naively subscribed to the 'get good grades, get a job, get a mortgage, have a family, retire, then die' dogma that is so fervently instilled into our impressionable youth. **At no point in my schooling was I taught how to start a company, file a tax return, invest successfully, or work towards financial freedom.** Great emphasis was placed on going to university - which I *eventually* did! - to earn a degree, as if my ideal, handsomely paid dream job would then magically materialise. This is not to berate university education - on the contrary, it has been a huge passion and rewarding career choice for me. At school however, starting a business and working for yourself just wasn't suggested as a realistic option. The stock market was perhaps fleetingly mentioned in history class, when we studied the Great Depression and the influence of John Maynard Keynes. One might expect that a principal **driver of wealth** and bellwether of a nation's economic standing would factor more heavily in the state education system, but this was simply not the case.

The school system fails children, in my opinion, by declining to establish the fundamentals of financial intelligence. In my case, I started learning about finance in my late twenties, almost by a stroke of luck. Nobody was there to teach me these concepts, but once I caught the

11

bug, I acquired knowledge primarily from books and the Internet. In English class, we studied Macbeth, Animal Farm and other classic works of literature. This was all fantastic, but what we didn't critique at school was **financial literature**, for instance *The Intelligent Investor* by Benjamin Graham, a legendary investor and mentor to none other than Warren Buffett, the most successful investor ever. In mathematics, we might have analysed and considered problems relating to stock valuation, or worked through *Security Analysis*, another classic by Benjamin Graham and David Dodd. The knowledge in these books and others can **literally make you a millionaire**, so why is this material not taught to kids?

These issues cemented my belief that there is an underlying agenda in the national curriculum. So many important facets of adult life are omitted from the school system, and children remain woefully unprepared to meet these challenges. These concerns include how to run an independent household, manage personal finances, set up a company, file a tax return, and so forth. Demonstrating real-world applications for mathematical ideas would surely promote engagement and interest? I was decidedly average at mathematics in school, but once I figured out how to apply some basic concepts my eyes were opened. If my teacher had told me **how the force of compounding could make me rich**, I might have sat up and listened a lot more.

It is my strong belief that concepts such as taxes, national insurance, pensions, assets, liabilities and equity should all be included in the national curriculum, with kids encouraged to discuss and debate these matters in their mid-late teenage years. If school is meant to prepare children for the adult world, perhaps there ought to be some representation of the monetary concerns of everyday adults within the syllabus? A sort of '*Finance 101*' for our young people would be ground-breaking and could equip them with the fiscal awareness to succeed in the wider world. Instead, schools are incredibly proficient at producing automatons for wage slavery, vassals that depend on a salary for most of their adult lives and lack the critical analysis and independence of thought necessary to become truly financially free.

First Employment and Adulthood

In contrast with a great swathe of my schoolmates, I made the decision not to go to university at 18 years old and got a job instead. I was tired of education and wanted cash in my pocket. I started my first 'proper' employment in a busy logistics office, initially as a warehouse stock controller and later as an apprentice delivery planner for 50-tonne trucks, or 'big rigs' for those of you in the United States. This experience was highly instructive, and a real shock to the system at that young age. I was now working in the adult world, with a diverse range of people and personalities. I had done menial work for pocket money during my early teens, but this was a different environment entirely.

What became readily apparent was that some of my colleagues had worked for the same company for all of their professional lives, and never tested the water anywhere else. Many were disillusioned and detested their jobs, but never made efforts to get themselves out of their situation and circumstances. They had **become trapped by their monthly salary** and titrated their outgoings to meet the costs of their lifestyle. Once their mortgage, car payments, utilities, television, broadband, and family needs were accounted for, nothing much was left in their bank account. In this way, they were stuck and would **never have the ability to become wealthy and financially free**. I lost count of how many people were holding out for their pension, hoping it would be the cure, a panacea, for all their ills. They were putting faith in someone else to look after their retirement (a pension fund manager) and just assuming that things would work out to their benefit in the end.

I knew that I didn't want to end up like many of my colleagues in their 40s, 50s and 60s, but had no idea at that time how to stop it from becoming a reality. I had started to loathe my job, the grind of the 9 - 5 rat race, and the mundane nature of the work. I felt that it didn't challenge me intellectually anymore and decided to consider my options. On one particular Monday morning, I lay in bed staring at the ceiling, dreading going to work, and thinking *'can I really do this for the rest of my life'*? Most successful people in the company, those with nice cars and suits that went to endless meetings (instead of throwing broken materials into a skip and moving pallets around) had all gone to university. At the time I believed this to be the best option for my future and made the journey back to full-time education, four years after I left.

Credit Crunch

Amid this personal and career backdrop, the initial months of my first job coincided with the build-up towards the real estate crash of 2007 - 2009, the largest recession since the Great Depression in the 1930s. This event was my first real exposure to the financial markets, and I distinctly remember my employer's stock price declining sharply. There was a palpable atmosphere of 'concerned malaise' in the workplace, and with hindsight it was a highly tumultuous time. If only I knew then what I do now, I could have deployed a decent amount of capital to buy attractively valued shares and be sitting on huge returns now in 2019. Funnily enough, I wish I'd purchased the depressed stock of my employer, **thus becoming an owner of my own productivity,** essentially a salaried owner of my company but on a much smaller scale. In more recent years, the stock has traded at a 35% discount to its net asset value and has a dividend yield of 8.3%! The business is still financially sound and produces modestly increasing cash flows on an annual basis. This analysis will make more sense after Part II, but it's interesting to look back on my personal history through the **prism of financial awareness.**

The nature of the financial crisis, its causes, and implications were completely lost on me back then. All I knew was that money would be tougher to come by in the housing market and in savings accounts, as interest rates were slashed to zero. Banks went from approving mortgages to anybody with a pulse at the height of the sub-prime lending era, to a wholesale tightening of the purse strings. This was after the government spent £500 billion of taxpayers' money **bailing them out of their own mess**. Savers would suffer for nearly a decade (and counting) as interest rates dropped to rock-bottom. Central banks used **quantitative easing** - essentially money printing - to increase liquidity and stimulate the economy. Only in the last 12 - 18 months have we seen interest rates in the USA and UK start to rise, after nearly a decade at virtually zero. Even now, the returns on government bonds and savings accounts are pitiful. Moreover, most of these assets provide a negative return after accounting for the impact of inflation and taxes. In other words, the **real rate of return is negative, and this is a disastrous outcome!**

Stock markets plummeted around the world, with the Standard and Poor's 500 (S&P 500) Index losing ~50% of its value in the 12-month period ending in November 2008. However, the markets were not affected equally across the globe, with China and India experiencing substantial growth during this period. It was the first time in my life that I came to comprehend the forces that manipulate the economy and financial markets - the large private institutions and central banks like the Federal Reserve and Bank of England. I started to tune in to prominent investors and their commentary; people like Peter Schiff of Euro Pacific Capital, who successfully predicted the financial crisis and warned about it several years before it took place. Although the wheels began to turn, I still wouldn't jump into the markets for a good while to come.

University and Academic Career

A large part of my decision to return to 'official' education was the hope that it would eventually provide meaningful, rewarding employment and an increased yet stable salary to that which I was accustomed. I had been interested in fitness, health and exercise for a long time and decided to commit to a degree in sport and exercise studies in 2009. It is still my firm belief that this was the best decision I could have made, given my circumstances at that time. I continued to work at weekends during my studies, until I was offered a redundancy deal in 2011 that I accepted. I was able to continue earning money for most of my degree, which arguably made my next step possible.

I managed to complete my undergraduate degree before tuition fees rocketed up to ~£9000 per year, and in general it was a highly enjoyable and rewarding experience. There were many helpful and knowledgeable tutors, and I made a couple of lifelong friends in the process. In my opinion, the most useful educational elements to emerge from my degree were critical analysis, and a preponderance towards rational and informed points of argument. It also taught me the value of independent study; of taking responsibility for my own future and **aligning the resources** at my disposal to *make things happen*. In contrast to the school classroom, in which knowledge is merely absorbed and then regurgitated in an exam or piece of coursework, university encouraged independent study and thought. These traits are indispensable for life in general but are particularly useful when valuing assets in the financial markets. The ability to **cut through the hype and irrelevant noise** is vitally important, and in retrospect my university education has made a lasting contribution in this area.

Following my undergraduate degree, I opted to pursue a postgraduate degree in sport and exercise nutrition. This would be the first time I had lived away from home and served as a great lesson in independence and personal responsibility. The degree itself was immensely rewarding and challenging, providing me with considerable opportunities for personal and academic growth. It would, however, come at a cost. I burned through all my savings within a 12-month period and took out a personal development loan from a bank to pay for my tuition fees. Although the degree itself and the two or three years that followed were immensely difficult, both mentally and financially, in the long run I believe that it was worth the risk. The postgraduate degree led to a teaching and research position that I held for two years. I was then able to commence a funded PhD scholarship in a topic of great personal interest to me.

After starting my PhD I made a concerted effort to pay down all of my debts, since I had a stable salary for the next few years, at least. I began with the largest amount first, which was my development loan. To do this effectively, I 'taxed' myself a specific sum each month and deducted it from my earnings on payday. As amounts were paid, I negotiated lower monthly payments while continuing to pay off the same sum, **compounding it down** until I could finally settle and be rid of it. I then sought to repay my mother who had made substantial monetary sacrifices to help me when I was in dire need of support. The whole experience was a great lesson - it taught me that **I never want to struggle again financially**.

I remember thinking that it would be great to have enough money to 'pay it forward' - in the words of Robert A. Heinlein - to pass on the generosity of others and help people in times of difficulty. I have a strong desire to reach a situation where I can do this at no great consequence, where money is no object and life can be truly open and free. Don't get me wrong I love working, but the ability to work out of enjoyment and not for the salary would be priceless. By applying the ideas and principles in the coming chapters, I will be able to make this a reality and you can too for yourselves and your families.

The Pursuit of Wealth: A Moral Conundrum?

The Highway to Freedom

In this day and age, the pursuit of wealth is regarded as anathema by contemporary society. In fact, I'd go as far as to suggest that the rich are pathologised in quite an overt sense. Somewhat paradoxically, it's not uncommon in the popular culture for people to aspire towards the 'Kardashian' lifestyle - one of being **famous for no appreciable reason** – or to be a contestant on Love Island, win the lottery and so on. Further examples of overnight success, without building anything of real substance from the ground up, are easily found in the Western world. In a society that holds instant gratification to such high esteem, this is not surprising. It's perfectly fine to desire fame and renown without incurring any sort of derogatory invective from the masses.

The unspoken commonality between all of these ambitions or 'careers' is the fame and, most importantly, **wealth that is a by-product of them**. It's extremely important to recognise this! Fame means *exposure*, which almost always equates to financial rewards, the extent of which depend on the impact that one has on the public consciousness. Using the Kardashians as an example, they are masters at using their popularity and influence among certain demographics for monetary gain. Whether you like them or not, this intuition and business savvy must be acknowledged and respected.

In contrast with the above examples, a great many celebrities simply burn out and disappear. Some squander their short-lived fortunes on frivolous entertainment, whereas others lose it on ill-advised investments and the like. In lacking the experience of building a significant fortune from scratch, over a lengthy period of time, these individuals **fail to respect the money that comes to them in a short time period and serve as poor custodians of it**. We see this especially with lottery winners, people that have won vast fortunes against all odds and then rapidly squandered it. Those that build wealth over the long term, following principles in line with those I'll be describing later, are cognisant of the time and effort it takes to accumulate money and tend to treat it with the necessary level of respect.

Given the perceived toxicity of wealth, why would someone pursue it in the first place? Moreover, what are the moral considerations of this? How does investing help create wealth? The major motivations, at least from my perspective, in seeking wealth are to enjoy the experiences life can bring. Notwithstanding social and emotional considerations, all the **best things in life cost money**, such as travelling, owning a sports car, running businesses, making gifts to charity, and so on. These pale into insignificance when you consider that the **greatest asset money can buy is freedom**. The ability to work because you want to, not because you have to; the freedom to travel wherever you want, whenever you want; and the option to stop exchanging your time for money in a job you don't enjoy.

Since the Great Recession we have seen the emergence of the Occupy Movement, amid widespread derision of big business, the capitalist system, income inequality and free market economics. This has worsened since the election of President Donald Trump in 2016.

Granted, in my late teens and early twenties I was sympathetic to many aspects of the Occupy agenda, and I've always been critical of *crony capitalism*. With that said, my political beliefs have evolved over the last decade towards more libertarian principles, with less consideration of left or right. **In my opinion, there is nothing to be gained by hating the rich and feeling sorry for your own circumstances.** The best way to mitigate such feelings is to do everything possible to change your lot in life, and there are multiple ways to bring this about. Once you have acquired resources and wealth you can then use them to change the world for the better and improve your own circumstances and those of the people around you.

Much has been said in recent times about taxing the rich and corporations more heavily, given the increasing gap between rich and poor. I'm not suggesting that the system we operate in is perfect, but this is erroneous thinking for several reasons. Firstly, on the issue of corporations, why should individuals be taxed twice on their business earnings? For example, a company will pay corporation tax on its profits at a rate of 19% in the United Kingdom, as of 2019. These earnings **belong to the shareholders of the company** and are managed by the Board of Directors on their behalf. Should they decide to pay out dividends from the distributable income, having retained enough in the business to meet capital requirements, each shareholder is likely to be taxed again on these dividends at the individual level. In the United Kingdom, if one receives more than £2000 in dividends per tax year, this income will be taxed at a rate of 7.5% for the lower rate band, maxing out at 38.1% in the higher rate band. If the shares are held in an individual savings account (ISA), the dividends will be shielded from tax. Nevertheless, it's easy to see the **double taxation** that is evident here, in that earnings from the same source are taxed twice.

In his legendary and influential text *Capitalism and Freedom* (2002), Nobel Prize-winning economist Milton Friedman (1912 - 2006) explains that a corporation is merely a vehicle to create wealth for shareholders, who can then do as they please with the cash that is generated. Without wealthy contributors, where would the capital investment originate? **The government does not create wealth, it only confiscates and redistributes it, nearly always with strings attached.** If a nation makes it unattractive for capital to reside within its borders, rich individuals can just leave the country, move their assets and take up residence in countries like Singapore or Hong Kong for instance, where assets can generate a more attractive return. The countries they leave behind are then left without the capital investment they might have otherwise benefited from. This impedes the productive capacity of the economy, and at the very worst leads to widespread economic depression. Capital investment is necessary to fund startup costs, purchase plant and other equipment, all under the premise of receiving a return on capital commensurate with the risk taken at the outset.

Morality and Greed

We hear much about the so-called 1%, the 'fat cats', or the super-rich, and most of it is negative, particularly when considering the role of the aforementioned Occupy Movement. In my opinion, **everyone should**

want to join the 1%, not destroy them. I'm not denying that there are morally bankrupt people in positions of wealth, power, and influence. It's important to note, however, that these individuals permeate our society at every level, be they a thief that robs a convenience store, or the payday loan companies that take advantage of people that don't know any better. The best-case scenario would be for a person to attain **financial abundance**, in that they possess the ways and means to change things in the world, and ally that with a strong moral compass to inform their decisions. Sadly, for every Warren Buffett, Bill Gates, and Ray Dalio there will always be a Robert Maxwell, Jordan Belfort or Bernie Madoff, and this is simply a fact of life. There will always be sketchy and repugnant individuals with vast finances, but **only you can decide to live life with morally sound principles** and use your resources for correspondingly virtuous objectives.

Another aspect that gets a lot of attention, particularly in the left-wing press, is the role of greed in our society. Gordon Gekko's famous 'Greed is Good' speech from the 1987 classic film *Wall Street* is often invoked to draw upon the negative connotations of greed. I would propose, however, that **greed is only a negative when it is underpinned by morally distasteful values**. For example, the accumulation of wealth for the sake of it, or the use of your resources to inflict pain and suffering on other people, are undoubtedly nefarious objectives. Contrastingly, it's clear that greed can be used in more upstanding ways. Would greed for knowledge hinder a keen and ambitious student? Would hunger and greed for wealth be a problem if it were used in a righteous manner, like donating more to charitable causes? The fundamental component of the equation is the moral basis of greed, and whether the individual is virtuous in their nature. Too often, the debate is oversimplified. It's easy to label all wealthy people as greedy without being fully aware of the facts, by making broad assumptions that they must have somehow disadvantaged people to achieve success. On the contrary, Warren Buffett, Bill Gates, Ray Dalio and many others have pledged to give away vast swathes of their personal fortunes to philanthropic causes when they pass on, according to The Giving Pledge. **As you focus on building wealth, be cognisant of why you're doing it from a moral and value-based perspective.**

My primary motivations are to **secure freedom** first and foremost, enjoy the full range of life experiences, and be able to give more to family, friends and charities. I am confident in the sound moral nature of these goals and simply need to take consistent, studious action to make them a reality.

The Spectre of Inflation

Inflation is regarded by most everyday people as 'the general increase in the price of goods and services' over a given period of time. This definition is partly true, but the underlying mechanisms for it are less well appreciated. Governments and central banks play a huge role in creating inflation, by **increasing the supply of currency beyond the rate of economic growth**. This brings about an increase in prices, but in actuality it is the erosion in purchasing power of the currency. Governments do this for a number of reasons, one being to pay off debt with devalued currency. Another is to fund programmes and spending without increasing taxes, which would be politically unpalatable for the voting public.

At the turn of the 20th century, the money supply in the United States and Great Britain was tied to gold reserves, the so-called 'gold standard'. In 1971 and 1931, respectively, these links were severed. The money we use today is thus referred to as 'fiat' currency - it is not backed by any particular commodity and the supply of it can be manipulated by central banks at their discretion. Several thinkers have referred to inflation as a **hidden tax**, and I agree with this description. If a government opts to engage in military conflict (as is liable to happen, and often under spurious motives), it's far easier to print the money - create it out of thin air - than levy huge tax increases on the populace. The pernicious effects of inflation, manifested in this manner, are not perceptible in the immediate term. Nevertheless, it's important to recognise that they do exist and will continue into the foreseeable future.

The government creates inflation, which increases the prices of assets, such as real estate and stocks. If said assets are sold and a capital gain is realised, the government taxes that as well. Therefore, we have the *covert* tax of inflation and *overt* tax on capital gains, **both working in unison**. It's a beautifully designed system, especially when you consider that the wage increases needed to maintain purchasing power often drag people into higher income tax thresholds[1]. In an ideal world, the money supply would be increased commensurate with the productive output of the economy, and not to excess. Instead, it's often businesses that bear the full brunt of the criticism for not increasing wages in line with inflation, when **the public ire should be directed at central banks and government**.

To illustrate the effects of inflation, let's use an example. If the rate of inflation is 3% per year, a product or service that costs £100 in Year 1 will cost £103 in Year 2, £106.09 in Year 3, £109.27 in Year 4, and so on. If your wages only increase by 2% each year, your money will have lost 1% of its purchasing power on an annual basis. This degradation over time is perhaps best illustrated by looking at the value of the US dollar expressed in gold - since 1947 the **dollar has lost nearly all of its purchasing power**[2].

When applied to savings and investments, it is absolutely essential to consider the impact of inflation on the nominal return of your assets. At present, most savings accounts in the United Kingdom

---

[1] https://www.bloomberg.com/news/articles/2019-04-04/higher-earners-in-britain-are-being-hit-by-stealth-tax-increases
[2] https://goldsilver.com/blog/purchasing-power-of-the-usd/

are still paying pitiful rates of interest (1 - 2% per annum), with rates only just beginning to rise. The situation is similar in the United States, with the Federal Reserve tentatively increasing rates in recent months. Therefore, I only recommend that you **use savings accounts for holding an emergency fund**, a pot of money that can cover your expenses for three months minimum, or preferably six months. This should be a suitable backstop if you were to lose your job or face similar extenuating circumstances. You still want to earn as much interest as possible from a savings account, to mitigate inflation to the best possible extent. In relation to your investments, the calculation of your **real rate of return** by adjusting for inflation, taxes and fees is an essential component in evaluating the performance of your portfolio.

Government and Pensions Won't Save You

I recently got into a heated debate on Facebook with a former schoolmate on the issue of retirement and the paltry future return of his State Pension. Let me be frank, if you're relying on the government to look after you in retirement, you're in for a big surprise. The state and public sector pension system in the UK - and many other countries for that matter - is best defined as an **intergenerational Ponzi scheme**.

When you make a contribution from your monthly salary, the funds *aren't invested*, they merely go into a huge pool of tax from which the presently eligible individuals collect their entitlements. Worse still, the funds might be spent on military entanglements or whatever concern the government deems appropriate. Thus, **the money is not compounded and there are no investment returns generated.** As you'll see later, the compounding of dividends or interest returns is a *fundamental component* in the pursuit of real wealth. From that perspective, the State Pension infrastructure is a complete farce, and in the coming years and decades the chickens will come home to roost. The ageing population will grow, and younger generations face the prospect of working harder and longer to slow the eventual implosion of the whole system. The declining birth rate will also place greater emphasis on the millennial generation to shoulder the burden[3]. Irrespective of this, more and more older adults are heavily reliant on the State Pension, holding

---

[3] https://www.theguardian.com/commentisfree/2018/oct/07/taxing-baby-boomers-will-create-better-fairer-britain-here-is-how

out for the day when they will be able to collect it, despite the paltry sum at the end.

There are notable exceptions to this flawed model around the world. Norway for example has reinvested its surplus petroleum profits into a Sovereign Wealth Fund that now totals ~$1 trillion in assets, or ~$195,000 per citizen. The fund is widely diversified and owns equities, bonds, and real estate assets that all generate returns, which are subsequently reinvested. There are several other countries with Sovereign Wealth Funds, such as Singapore, that serve as additional examples of nations with prudent financial planning. Norway is also noteworthy in that it has recorded budget surpluses for many years, whereas the UK and USA have run up substantial deficits.

Allow me to illustrate just how pitiful the State Pension is in the UK. To qualify for a State Pension, you must pay National Insurance contributions for a period of at least 10 years but need to contribute for 35 years to get the full amount possible. Assuming you could retire tomorrow, your State Pension entitlement would be £164.35 per week, or £8,528 per annum, **which is an abysmal return for a lifetime of labour.** The money is locked up and frozen until you reach the eligible age (which is subject to increase)[4] and when payments begin they are factored in with your taxable income. This amount is **insufficient to support even a basic standard of living**. Your reward for paying National Insurance - which is a tax, the government takes it by force - is not even enough to cover your living expenses. So, we have established

---

[4] https://www.theguardian.com/money/2018/oct/09/state-pension-age-rise-thousands-women-london-protest

that the government is not to be relied on if our desire is to attain financial abundance, and why should we be surprised?

Let's also consider company (or workplace) pensions, which are an inherently better bet, despite some evident flaws. A major plus for company pensions is the fact that your employer also contributes to the scheme, and the funds you pay in aren't subject to income tax. The money is still under lock and key, until you reach the age of 55. After this point, you may withdraw some or all of the fund, with the first 25% tax-free and the rest taxed as income. Therefore, a careful decision must be made as to how much you withdraw as a lump sum and how much you preserve for regular income.

I have a couple of pensions from both present and prior employment. The first is a scheme from my first ever job at 18, until I left three years later. As you might expect, it hasn't made me a millionaire! This pension has since been frozen until 2043 but will nevertheless continue to accumulate at a tepid rate. The scheme is invested in a UK equity index fund that tracks the FTSE All-Share Index, comprising approximately 600 of the 2000 or so companies that trade on the London Stock Exchange. I have a number of concerns with this structure. Firstly, the majority of the fund is denominated in Pound Sterling; there is limited exposure to other currencies and this can serve as an important inflation hedge. Moreover, if the UK market were to crash at an inopportune moment, one could lose a huge amount of money just as they need it to live on. Hence, international exposure is a crucial part of diversification for maximising returns and minimising risk.

As monthly contributions are made to a pension, you are essentially 'buying the market' at whatever price it is currently trading at, without any discretion or due diligence. Furthermore, any income thrown off by the fund is reinvested, irrespective of the price. The fund is ring-fenced until age 55, which is preferential to the State Pension threshold, but still patronising to responsible and prudent investors that want to take ownership and control for themselves.

In the UK, there is a lifetime pension allowance of £1.03 million, with any pension savings over this threshold taxed at 55% (lump sum) or 25% (cash withdrawals). **This sum is not a huge amount if you want to really enjoy your retirement.** People that have worked all their lives and put money into pensions in good faith should not have to scrimp and compromise. It should be a time for enjoyment and reward, sampling everything that life has to offer, and living in abundance that can then be passed on to your children, a charity, or some other trust as **part of your legacy.**

To this end, I would much rather take personal responsibility by **building my own nest egg and choosing my own investments**, whilst minimising fees and tax. I advise that you make use of employer contributions to whatever pension scheme you have in place and contribute the requisite monthly amount. However, you should recognise that with State and workplace pensions, you are placing your financial future at the whim of the government, the central bank, and the pension manager. It's much more desirable to educate yourself and take personal responsibility for your monetary affairs, so that you can maintain your self-determination and freedom.

Investing and Speculation: An Important Distinction

We have established the nature of investing and the rationale behind it in the previous chapters. As I alluded to in the introduction, my fundamental ideas about stocks and shares have not always been congruent with these principles. My perspective was framed by films like Oliver Stone's 1987 classic *Wall Street*, or the more recent 2015 film *The Big Short*. Both of these titles are superb pieces of cinema and I highly recommend them, but they may put across some **discordant messages for passive income investors.**

In *Wall Street*, the narrative focuses on the buying and selling of stocks within a short time frame to capitalise on price movements. This activity is **speculation** not investing - the act of purchasing a stock solely on the basis that its price will increase. I made this mistake when I first started and will describe this in more detail later. The film's legendary antagonist, Gordon Gekko, carries out certain trades using *insider information*, a criminal offence in many jurisdictions. Therefore, it's easy to draw the wrong conclusions from this albeit classic film. Capitalising on short-term price movements in stocks is only really meaningful with huge trades, requiring large amounts of capital, and trading within this time frame has been made largely irrelevant due to the emergence of **high-frequency trading and algorithms**. For the novice investor with limited capital, the practice of short-term trading is a fool's gambit, and best left well alone.

More recently, *The Big Short* dramatises the real-world experiences of individuals that profited from the 2008 financial crisis and sub-prime collapse by betting that mortgage-backed securities would fall in value. To accomplish this, they 'shorted' the housing market using complex financial instruments called credit default swaps. These instruments and other 'derivatives' track the value of an asset, or security, *without actually owning the underlying asset*. That is to say, the price of the derivative is intrinsically tied to the performance of something else, hence the name. These complicated instruments are outside the remit of the novice investor and certainly **beyond the scope of this book**.

There have been several speculative asset bubbles in living memory, but two still reside within the public consciousness**. The tech boom of the late 1990s and housing bubble of the mid-2000s are two primary examples of speculation in action.** In the former, cash poured into the stock market and prices were inflated to extremely high levels. Technology and internet stocks were particularly in vogue, and were ridiculously overvalued by anyone's set of assumptions. Many of these companies were yet to post anything resembling earnings. Nobody knew what they actually did or whether they would be profitable in the future. It was utter mania, and Wall Street was only too happy to enable this insanity. Companies like Enron were lauded with buy ratings from a host of analysts, even as the stock price plummeted from $90 per share to $1 per share, over an 18-month period. This was due in part to the insanity of the bubble, fraud, and the stark conflict of interest between Wall Street analysts and the company. Enron **never paid a dividend**, so those that bought in at the high didn't make a penny from the stock. Indeed, shareholders lost billions and it remains one of the great scandals in US stock market history.

The 'dotcom' bubble burst in the early 2000s and money made its way into real estate. People were buying houses under the mistaken premise that property prices would rise in perpetuity. I detailed some elements of this bubble and the wider economic crash in earlier chapters. I can distinctly remember the media enthusiasm and that of everyday people who thought that the key to generating wealth was taking a mortgage out on a home, sitting back, and letting the property appreciate to sell out at a profit. Certainly, a great number of people made money with property speculation prior to the recession, but prevailing wisdom dictated that the bubble would never burst. When it did, huge sums were lost and many individuals that had sat out the mania were only too glad to swoop in and buy attractive real estate at bargain prices.

More recently, the cryptocurrency phenomenon, although distinctly separate from the stock market, serves as another example of rampant speculation. People buy Bitcoin, Ethereum and others on the basis that they will go up in value, **without the promise of any cash flow during the holding period**. This isn't the case with dividend stocks, bonds or rental property. A cursory look at the Bitcoin price over the last few years reveals its hugely volatile nature. At the right moment, it was possible to buy in and realise great profits, if you had the discipline to sell out. It was also possible to lose vast sums if you were a late arrival to the scene, or held on too long, especially given the recent irrational swings in price during 2018 for example.

I'm **not suggesting that speculation is innately wrong**, it's just riskier than investing for cash flow. What's more, in a standard, tax-liable brokerage account, any shares that are sold are likely to be subject to Capital Gains Tax. Even in an ISA or Roth IRA, there are charges and commissions associated with buying and selling stocks, and these can add up, especially in the beginning. **If you are dealing with sums in the hundreds of pounds per trade, the impact of regularly trading positions will be greatly magnified and erode your returns.** In addition to this, a lot of stocks in growth sectors don't pay dividends. In other words, they **don't throw off passive income**, which is the whole point of the strategy presented in this book.

There is no doubt that the big technology companies of recent years have offered tremendous growth and created vast wealth for investors that got in at the right time. The FAANG stocks (Facebook, Amazon, Apple, Netflix, and Alphabet/Google) have all grown tremendously, but towards the latter end of 2018 the market seemed to be pulling back from them. Amazon passed a market capitalisation of $1 trillion, which is a phenomenal achievement of course. I still wouldn't buy the stock, because the framework of a **passive income strategy** doesn't permit it. The company is a behemoth and it has fundamentally changed the world, but it pays no dividends. I don't want to have to sell an ownership stake in a company to realise profits. I would much rather share in the earnings, which as a shareholder *I'm entitled to anyway.* Indeed, an ownership mentality is absolutely integral to long-term investing, but this is anathema to speculators and those that trade within a short time frame. By following a long-term strategy, you are positioning yourself as an owner and investor, as opposed to a trader or speculator. Moreover, you hold passive income as sacrosanct and a bedrock principle of your investment strategy.

The Power of Compounding: Building Cash Flow

Most people are aware of the principle of compounding, but few truly understand what it means in practice. Albert Einstein is said to have called it 'the eighth wonder of the world' and 'the greatest mathematical discovery of all time'. Whether apocryphal or not, these statements highlight the importance of **reinvesting your passive income streams**. 'Simple' interest, in which the returns are spent for instance, differs hugely from 'compound' interest where returns are **reinvested into other income-yielding assets**. This concept is extremely powerful and is a fundamental truth that should be taught to everyone in school, but sadly this is not the case. The principles of passive income and compounding are the central tenets of the investment strategy put forward in this book and an understanding of these mechanisms is key.

The essence of compounding is the **reinvestment of cash flows** - for example interest in a savings account or dividends from stocks - so that the investor generates **returns on returns**. Cash sitting in your bank account is dying due to the pitiful interest rates; it's far better to keep it alive by redeploying it to earn more for you. When you first start out this process is rather difficult, as the income return is very small. However, it gets easier as time progresses. Eventually, **exponential growth takes place**, with new principal churning out more and more cash. The key in the early days is patience, discipline, and possessing the clarity of mind to stay on course towards your end goal. With simple interest, a 30-year investment of £10,000 at a yield of 6% would return £18,000 of cash, plus the principal of £10,000 if we disregard capital appreciation. When returns are compounded, this amount would be the considerably larger sum of £57,435, including the initial principal.

For your own calculations, the formula for compounding can be expressed as $a*(1 + r)t$, where a is the initial principal, r is the percentage rate of return, and t is the number of time periods where the returns have been reinvested. **Differences of one percentage point of return can pose huge implications** for compounding when viewed over the long term. Let me illustrate the point using our previous example. Over a 30-year period, let's say we invest £10,000 at a yield of 6%, with all income reinvested at the same rate on an annual basis, without adding any more capital. Disregarding capital gains through share price increases, our final amount after 30 years would be £57,435. The same amount invested at a rate of 5% would return a total of £43,219 after the same duration, following the same assumptions. Hopefully this illustrates the **crucial impact of both compounding and the rate of return** for your investments.

A simple rule of thumb for calculating roughly how long it takes to **double your money** with compounding is the so-called **'Rule of 72'**. In short, you divide the rate of return, let's say 10%, into 72, which gives 7.2 years to double your money. For a rate of 6% this would be 12 years, so the impact of percentage return is felt in both the time it takes to double your principal, and the final sum at the end of the investment period. **These assumptions are based on one initial investment sum, with no further additions of capital.** If the investor continues to make regular contributions to the cash flow machine, it's easy to understand how the compounding effect can be magnified. What's more, when you factor in dividend growth and yield on cost (to be discussed later) the effects can be enhanced to an even greater extent. These calculations don't account for inflation, taxes and fees of course, and these need to be comprehended to understand the *real rate of return*.

Another important thing to consider is that companies can compound money themselves, in a way that bonds and real estate cannot. After accounting for dividend payments, the leftover earnings in a successful business are retained and deployed for expansion and growth. Should this happen in a desirable manner, **greater distributions will be possible in the future**, and this usually coincides with share price increases as well.

Developing an Ownership Mindset

The cultivation of an ownership mentality is a crucial aspect of investing for passive income, especially over the long term. Instead of merely existing as a consumer within the political, economic and social system; investing allows you to **own pieces of the infrastructure that supports the society you live in**. Consider all the sectors that play a role in your daily life, for example insurance, oil and gas, utilities, raw materials, housing and property, just to name a few. You spend your hard-earned money every month on goods and services that are generally required or desired, so why shouldn't you take an ownership stake in the businesses that stand to profit from these transactions?

As an example, imagine that your energy supplier decides to increase your bills by 7%. The causes and motivations for this on their part are numerous, but let's say they blame it on increases in wholesale energy prices. A *consumer* of energy would understandably be annoyed at such an increase and curse the impact on their household finances. They might even switch their energy supplier to a cheaper one, and in many cases, this is a sensible strategy to adopt. However, as an *owner* of the energy company, you would be less concerned about such an increase, as this would likely coincide with **greater earnings for your company**, a proportional share of which you **would be entitled to**. This example can be applied to many other sectors, such as oil and gas, insurance and mortgages, and so forth. As prices increase to mitigate the punitive effects of inflation, owners of businesses can minimise these unwelcome effects. Fuel may be more expensive at the pump, but if you own shares in Exxon Mobil or Royal Dutch Shell, the cash outflow from your current account eventually makes its way to your company's income statement and balance sheet. If you **regard yourself as an owner of a business**, no matter how small your piece of the pie, it will stand you in good stead as a passive income investor.

When a proportion of earnings are paid out as dividends (see Part II), this action can be regarded as **taking a profit on the back end.** Many businesses serve an essential need for us to maintain our quality of life, so why not share in their success? The increase in prices, concomitant with an increased dividend payout, will result in more earnings being retained in the business for future compounding. A dividend that rises in line with inflation - **or ideally in excess of it** - will enable reinvestment in more company stock or allow the investor to deploy the capital elsewhere in more attractive opportunities. In addition, some companies have shareholder perks that can be exploited, such as deals, coupons, vouchers and the like, that all make stock ownership even more enticing. Above all, you should distance yourself from the view that stocks are just financial instruments or lines on a screen, and instead cultivate a mindset that you are buying real, functional businesses.

This ownership attitude should be reflected in your actions. By being a proactive and interested investor, you should be reading financial statements, earnings reports and presentations of companies within your sphere of interest. You may potentially attend annual general meetings to vote on matters related to your holdings and tune in to earnings calls. In the 21st century, information on public companies has never been more freely available and you should foster a keen enthusiasm in this respect. The process of stock selection and appraisal will be explored later in Part II, and an ownership perspective is integral to this analysis.

Be Clear on Assets and Liabilities

Too often, people confuse what an asset is and what a liability is. In the simplest terms, an asset is something that generates a return for you, or puts money in your pocket every month, as Robert Kiyosaki likes to say. Contrastingly, a liability is something that costs you money each month. Therefore, an asset would be something like a **dividend-paying stock**, a bond, savings account or rental property. A liability would be a car loan, mortgage, credit card, taxes, insurance and the like. To help you in your goal of financial abundance, you need to **minimise liabilities as much as possible.** The government and others with conflicting interests would prefer that you don't!

Unsecured debt in the UK has spiralled out of control since the 2008 crash, rising almost 50% to £15,385 per household[5]. **Consumption should be fuelled by wages and surplus investment income, not credit cards and debt.** We all know people that fund a lifestyle they can't afford with credit cards and overdraft facilities. What people should do instead is live within their means and postpone lavish spending until they are in a more stable financial position. This can be extremely difficult, as people with no debt tend to be bombarded with emails and literature encouraging them to take on debt!

---

[5] https://www.theweek.co.uk/98778/what-is-the-average-uk-household-debt

Somewhat contrastingly, debt within the structure of a limited liability company is less of a worry, as the **individual is not personally exposed to the debt**. Private companies can use debt to help expand their business and bring about growth, without leaving the directors insolvent should the company go under. This is not the case when taking out **personal** loans, credit cards and mortgages for instance. You are liable to make the payments every month, rain or shine, and if you default you could end up insolvent.

It's very useful to get into the practice of listing your assets and liabilities on a monthly or bimonthly basis. By subtracting your liabilities from your assets, you can calculate your **equity**. For example, if you have £10,000 in a savings account but a £6,000 loan on a car, your equity is £4,000. Hence, if you pay down the debt or add to your savings and investments, your equity will rise. A rising equity over time **is hugely desirable** because it means you are exchanging your time and labour for something in return. Too many people swap their productivity for very little and end up dipping into their overdraft at the end of each month. By being mindful of this simple equation, you can gain control of your household finances but also understand, at a rudimentary level, the finances of the companies you are interested in buying shares in.

Getting Started: Taking the Reins

Stock Market Basics

In simple terms, stock markets enable the trading of financial instruments called stocks, shares or *equities* on a public exchange. These exchanges list common stocks (sometimes called equity shares in the United Kingdom) as well as debt instruments like corporate bonds. These exchanges are situated in most of the developed economies around the world, in countries that allow private ownership of the means of production.

Imagine a large and successful business as a huge brick wall. Each brick represents one share of ownership in the company, and every day hundreds of thousands, even millions, of bricks are transacted on these public exchanges. Virtually all of these transactions are completed using electronic means. Companies list on exchanges around the world to raise capital for growing their business. In doing so, they must disclose a considerable amount of previously unavailable information and undergo regulatory oversight. The stock market environment provides liquidity, in that it's easy to buy and sell shares without drastically affecting the price of the asset or security being traded.

By participating in the system, you can own a very small piece, relatively speaking, of these companies and participate in their success or failure. Through investing in the market, you are basically **sacrificing short-term satisfaction and enjoyment for prosperity in the future**. This attitude might be anathema to the youth of today - those that have been encouraged to spend (i.e., consume) in a low interest rate environment - but it's an indispensable perspective that should underpin your investing mindset.

The great thing about many stocks is that they serve as an important **hedge against the effects of inflation**. Take gold-mining stocks for instance - as the price of gold increases due to the declining value of currency, profits and cash flow increase, leading to capital gains and dividend growth. Consumer staples such as PepsiCo and General Mills can increase their prices incrementally, and we hear about this all the time in the mainstream media. If inflation is high these blue-chip stocks tend not to be affected and **continue earning vast profits even during recessionary periods**.

Finding a Broker

The first step towards building a stock portfolio is to choose a broker. Your shares and their respective certificates will all be held in this electronic 'basket' so to speak. Each broker has their own costs for holding your shares - a 'platform charge' - alongside **costs for carrying out transactions (buying or selling shares)**. In addition to the brokerage costs involved, there may also be nuances to the interface that are important to consider. I switched from my first broker after a short while because their website menus and data were appalling to look at and difficult to navigate. When you are conducting regular research and analysis on different stocks, the **efficacy of the brokerage platform is a crucial element**. Do your due diligence in finding the most cost effective and accessible brokerage platform, as you will be using it on a regular basis over a period of many years.

Another element that is often neglected is the level of access your prospective broker has to the financial markets. In the United Kingdom, some brokers only have access to the London Stock Exchange, and perhaps some selected stocks in Europe and North America. I'll discuss international exposure later, but it's important to bear in mind the level of access that a broker will provide and how that reconciles with their total costs. For example, the broker I currently use provides access to the UK market as well as several exchanges on the European continent and North America. They don't provide the opportunity to buy individual stocks on exchanges in the Far East and Asia-Pacific regions, but I can circumvent this to some extent by purchasing index or exchange-traded funds in these localities. It's also possible to hold brokerage accounts in individual countries in these regions, such as Singapore or Hong Kong, where you can research and purchase individual stocks, but more on that later.

It is **extremely important to minimise the tax obligations of your investments**. To this end, I would strongly recommend setting up a stocks and shares ISA (individual savings account) if you are based in the United Kingdom. In the United States, this would be similar to setting up a Roth IRA (individual retirement account). If you receive a taxable salary and have your emergency fund in place, it's vital that you **max out a tax-free account first** before opening a second investment account. Presently, a stocks and shares ISA allows you to put in £20,000 per year and acts as a tax-free basket for these funds. Anything that you buy within this basket will not be subject to capital gains tax (for example if you sell some stock for more than you bought it for) and any income you receive in the way of dividends or interest will be tax-free as well. Therefore, to stop taxes from eroding your investment returns it's integral that you max out your ISA contribution each year before opening an additional (tax-liable) investment account.

Once you've signed up for a brokerage account, you can start to move disposable cash into it each month. I like to 'tax' myself when I get my monthly salary and move the cash straight over to my brokerage account. The amount you should transfer depends on your monthly cash flows, but nevertheless you should move what you can in anticipation of making a stock purchase. You also need to consider a buffer for your account, to meet the cost of fees. These charges are taken monthly and depend on the amount of money you have under management with your broker. Mine currently charges 0.49% on an annual basis, with a cap of £45 per year.

Congratulations, you have successfully set up a brokerage account! The next step is to **add your first stock**, one with sound fundamentals and **income-generating capacity**.

PART II
Stock Selection and Valuation Principles

Dividends: The Cornerstone

Dividends are perhaps the most fundamental principle underlying the investment thesis put forward in this book. Put simply, dividends are cash that is paid to investors as a reward for owning the stock of a company. As an investor, **you share in the success of a business by receiving a percentage of its earnings**, based on the number of shares you currently hold. Dividends are driven by underlying business prosperity and success, **not market sentiment or emotion.** Indeed, last year UK-listed firms paid out record dividends, totalling almost £100 billion, despite the FTSE 100 index experiencing its worst year for a decade[6]. What's more, these payouts are expected to be surpassed in 2019, both in the UK[7] and around the world[8].

Sadly, it is not dividends and their growth, but rather share prices and their movements that are the focal point of mainstream media and public interest at large. All we hear about in the news is the movement of indices such as the S&P 500 or FTSE 100, and this is regrettable. Depending on the source data and time period, dividends and compounding are **historically responsible for around 50 – 70% of the total stock market return**, which is ridiculous! In this chapter, I will hopefully illustrate how dividends drive portfolio performance and

---

[6] https://www.theguardian.com/business/2019/jan/21/shareholders-received-record-dividends-of-almost-100bn-in-2018-brexit
[7] https://uk.finance.yahoo.com/news/income-investing-alert-uk-dividends-152859084.html
[8] http://www.morningstar.co.uk/uk/news/172003/global-dividends-hit-new-record.aspx

wealth accumulation. I'll also explain what to look for when assessing the viability of a dividend-paying stock.

Companies can do several things with their 'bottom-line' earnings - the cash that is left after deducting taxes, expenses, and the cost of goods sold. These might include putting the cash in the bank, reinvesting for further expansion, returning capital to shareholders with dividends, paying down debt, buying back stock on the market, or acquiring other companies. The management of most publicly-traded, dividend-paying businesses will make a commitment to pay dividends on an annual, semi-annual, quarterly, or even a monthly basis. A dividend is usually agreed by the board at the AGM (Annual General Meeting) and approved before it is formally announced. Sometimes, management will announce 'special' dividends. These are one-off payments on top of the usual payment schedule and are generally less predictable, but always welcome!

In tandem with the dividend announcement, the *record* date and *ex-dividend* date will be made clear in press materials and on the company website. Purchasing a stock on or after the so-called ex-dividend date means that the buyer has lost the right to receive the dividend; and instead this right is conferred on the seller of the stock. If you buy the stock before this date, you will be paid the per-share dividend amount on the *dividend payment date* into your brokerage account. This cash is then available for you to buy more stock in the same company, a more attractively valued business, or you can spend it how you please. Do keep in mind that **if the dividends are spent you lose the ability to**

compound these cash flows, and this is vital for wealth accumulation over time.

I don't deny that it's possible to make money through capital appreciation - the increase in market value of your shareholdings - via business growth, expansion and the subsequent recognition of this by the markets in the share price. This is also true of share buybacks, when companies use cash to buy their own shares on the market and then liquidate them. This results in an increase in available earnings and dividends on a per-share basis, which should correspond with higher market valuations. However, to realise market gains **one must relinquish their ownership stake in the company by selling shares**, which might mean exiting a position in a well-run, successful, cash flow-generative enterprise. If your shares are not sheltered in an ISA or similar, the appreciation that is realised when you sell a position will be vulnerable to Capital Gains Tax, whereas dividend payments are usually subject to lower taxes under the same circumstances. Remember that **earned income is always taxed at a greater rate than investment income!**

The best thing about dividends is that they are cash flows into your account and can be spent as you please. They can be used in times of need to support the payment of household bills for instance, and this cannot be achieved by owning stocks like Amazon **that don't yield income at present**. Furthermore, dividends keep the company management honest. It's very difficult to lie about your financial position if you have to distribute cold, hard cash to shareholders. This demonstrates that earnings are real, and rewards shareholders for taking the risks that correspond with stock ownership. Stocks that don't pay dividends tend to be much more volatile, and it's only really possible to make money by exiting a position, assuming someone is there to buy your shares from you.

Payment History

A long dividend history is **perhaps the most compelling evidence that a company is profitable**, and this allied with dividend growth is indicative of a successful and prosperous business. For example, Colgate-Palmolive, Procter and Gamble, and Exxon Mobil have all paid dividends for well over a century. They may not have increased their payments each and every year, but they have all maintained their dividends through thick and thin. This is primarily due to the strength of their business models and fundamental role in society. Another example is the Canadian Imperial Bank of Commerce, which hasn't missed a regular dividend payment since 1868![9] These payments have generally grown over the years, but were held constant during the Great Recession of 2008, along with those of many other established companies.

The regular distribution of cash to shareholders has the effect of holding management's feet to the fire, because if cash flow can't support the dividend it betrays the fundamental health of the business. There can be no distortions or weasel words in a company's income statements or annual reports if there is a commitment to deliver distributions.

---

[9] https://www.cibc.com/en/about-cibc/investor-relations/share-information/common-share-information/common-dividends.html

In the tech boom of the late 1990s, companies like Enron weren't paying dividends and shareholders in general didn't want them. Many people at the time were buying stocks purely on the assumption that they would go up in price, **a completely speculative pursuit** given that most of the businesses were unsustainable, and nobody could work out how they made money! Stocks were trading at hundreds of times their net asset value or earnings. The tremendous recent success and popularity of the so-called FAANG stocks - Facebook (FB), Amazon (AMZN), Apple (AAPL), Netflix (NFLX), and Alphabet (GOOG) - certainly feels like history repeating itself. Back then, Wall Street convinced people that they didn't need dividends and should buy stocks solely on the premise that they would increase in price, irrespective of the financial health or prospects of the underlying businesses themselves. This nonsensical assumption, as with the housing bubble that followed, relied on the proviso that somebody would be there to buy the stocks from you, so that you could eventually take the profits. **The ideal stock is the one you can buy and own forever**, that keeps throwing off incremental cash flow, and has lasting prosperity and success.

If a company cuts its dividend, as General Electric has recently, this is **a major red flag** and a signifier that the health of the company is in decline. This is a signal to sell the stock and consider an alternative company that is attractively valued and offers a nice yield. Real opportunities lie in purchasing stocks that are out of favour, for matters unrelated to the fundamentals of the business, thereby allowing the prospective investor to **buy the right to incremental cash flows at a bargain price**. The trick is in finding these opportunities and ensuring (to the best of your ability) that the cash flows are sustainable for the long term.

Yield

One of the major metrics of interest to income investors is the current dividend yield. This is calculated by dividing the annual dividend per share (the dividend paid over the last 12 months) by the current share price. Let's use a simple example and calculate current yield as follows:

6p [annual dividend] / 100p [current share price] = 0.06 * 100 = **6%**

This would suggest a **great starting yield for a business**, and if we were to make a stock purchase now this would 'lock in' our yield at that price, assuming the dividend were held at that rate. This starting yield is substantially higher than that currently available in savings accounts, and rightly so given the extra risk we're taking by owning the stock. Ideally, the dividend yield needs to be higher than the 10-year government bond rate, to justify the risk we're taking. If we could receive the same yield by lending money to the government (i.e., UK gilts, US Treasury notes or bonds), this would be the obvious and preferential choice. Remember, we as shareholders have **the residual claim** on the company's assets, meaning that if the company goes under the debtholders get paid first, and we, the shareholders, get the leftovers if there are any. For assuming this risk, we must be compensated with dividends. In our example, the yield is extremely attractive, especially if the company is established and has good cash flow generation. However, there are other metrics we need to consider as well before considering a hypothetical purchase.

Growth Rate

The starting yield of our example stock is fantastic on its own, providing us with a 6% dividend return, irrespective of any share price increases on top of that. However, let's suppose **the business has a solid commitment to dividend growth over time**, with an average dividend growth rate of 15% over the last 5 years. Projected into the future, our initial yield of 6p per share could balloon to an annual payment of 12p in 5 years, just by holding the stock! This can't be guaranteed and depends on the underlying success of the business and earnings growth. The compounding of the dividend, allied to reinvestment of these cash flows, is **key to driving portfolio performance and wealth.** The value of this concept is explained further below, in the discussion on **yield on cost.**

Sustainability

Alongside the dividend yield and its growth rate, we also need to ensure that **the dividend is sustainable over time**. If a company is paying out more than it earns annually in dividends, it doesn't take a rocket scientist to understand that this is not a recipe for financial health. Company directors will do their utmost not to cut the dividend, but if this is a fundamental necessity a drop in the share price will usually result. The

payout ratio is the annual dividend divided by the earnings per share (EPS) and expressed as a percentage. Going back to our example, let's say our company earns 12p per annum, and work out the payout ratio:

6p [annual dividend] / 12p [earnings per share] = 0.5 * 100 = **50%**

In simple terms, this means that the company pays out 50% of its earnings in dividends to shareholders. This calculation can also be presented as dividend cover (the amount of times the dividend is covered by earnings) by dividing the EPS by the dividend per share. For our example the dividend is covered twice by earnings. Many companies will state a commitment with regards to the payout ratio. For example, the Bank of Montreal has a policy of paying out 40 – 50% of its earnings as dividends to shareholders over time.[10] Given that earnings are likely to increase annually, we can expect concomitant increases in dividends as well.

A complete picture needs to be built up with regards to yield, growth and sustainability during the stock selection process. It's no good picking a stock with a yield in excess of 10% if there is no growth and the payout considerably exceeds EPS. This would suggest that the company is using cash reserves or debt to make dividend payments – **a recipe for disaster** – and heralds a dividend cut. These stocks represent so-called 'dividend traps' and it's important to watch out for them.

---

[10] https://www.bmo.com/home/about/banking/investor-relations/shareholder-information/dividend-information

The Importance of Yield on Cost

We have successfully established the principles of dividend yield, growth and sustainability for portfolio performance and total returns. Alongside these concepts, the role of yield on cost (YOC) is paramount for income investors to understand. Unfortunately, this metric is lost in the public discourse about stocks and the financial markets. Like much of investing, **its impact is felt over the long term** and is relatively imperceptible year-on-year, but nevertheless it holds the key to financial abundance.

To illustrate, let's assume we buy 500 shares of our example business at 100p per share, for a transaction cost of £500 (not including fees and taxes). This will entitle us, at present, to receive 6p of income per share, or £30 in annual dividends. Over the years the dividend will probably rise – remember we established that the dividend per share could swell to 12p in five years? This £60 of annual income in Year 5 will represent a **yield on cost of 12%!** That is, we will receive at least 12% of our initial investment cost each year, provided the dividend is maintained from that point. These payments will continue to grow over the years, until we eventually receive more than the initial share transaction each year **in dividends alone!** This is the **life-changing power of investing in stocks** but is a concept that very few lay people are aware of. The preponderance of the media to focus on stock price movements (as opposed to dividend payments and their growth) is surely responsible for this folly.

The relationship between yield on cost and the present dividend yield can be quite informative. If there is a substantial difference between the two, for instance if the present yield is much lower than the YOC we can assume that capital appreciation has taken place. The extent of the difference could inform a decision to sell the stock and realise a profit, but if the dividend is not in danger why should we bother? Instead, we might be better off continuing to hold the stock. In this way, we benefit from a growing yield on cost, which is perhaps one of the most important elements of income investing to consider over the long-term.

Market Valuation

Alongside the dividend calculations that are all-important, there are several measures investors need to understand that relate to the market value of the prospective business. These are by no means exhaustive, but rather serve as some of the key indicators that should be used in conjunction with dividend-specific considerations.

Price-Earnings Ratio

Often known as the earnings multiple, this ratio is expressed as the company share price (available on a consistent basis almost anywhere) divided by the EPS. In simple terms, it illustrates how much investors are willing to pay for £1 of earnings (or whatever currency your domestic market is denominated in). For example, if a company is trading at a multiple of 20, it means that investors are willing to pay £20 per share of stock in a company with an EPS of £1. If the share price doubles but earnings remain the same, you would be paying £40 for the same £1 of earnings.

I prefer to take the average earnings from the previous five years or preferably more (if available) to account for any irregularities in earnings and calculate a P/E ratio from this average using the current share price. This can then be compared to companies in the same sector and the broader market - this information is widely available online, for instance on the Morningstar website. Using the criteria of value investing legend Benjamin Graham, we can regard a stock trading at a multiple of

<10 as cheap, 10 - 20 as moderately priced, and >20 as expensive. More importantly, we should compare the P/E to other companies in the same sector as well as the general market, alongside the historical average.

A company trading at a sky-high P/E tends to reflect that a stock is overvalued, or that there are assumptions for high growth in the business. Thinking back to the dot-com boom, many technology companies were trading at huge P/E ratios, reflecting the emotion-driven, inflated prices of these stocks. Today, Amazon trades at a P/E of around 92, which is extremely high even when considering its phenomenal growth. A consequence of this is that earnings must grow rapidly to catch up with the market valuation, and if earnings miss consensus estimates the stock price can get hit hard.

By calculating the P/E using earnings from the previous year, we can work out the trailing P/E. By contrast, we can calculate a forward P/E using expected earnings for the following year. Personally, I don't like to make assumptions about expected earnings, as these can be way off the mark, and instead use earnings from prior years. This information can be found on the company website or the financials section of your brokerage platform. Going back to our hypothetical example, the trailing P/E ratio would be as follows:

100p [share price] / 12p [trailing annual EPS] = **8.3x**

By using a combination of five-year average and trailing P/E, we can begin to build up a picture of the market valuation of the stock in question.

A lesser used metric that can be derived from the P/E ratio is the **earnings yield**. This is the inverse of the P/E ratio and can be calculated for our example as follows:

12p [trailing EPS] / 100p [share price] = 0.12 * 100 = **12%**

This yield can be compared to prevailing interest rates (which are at historic lows) to suggest the return of the investment. In our case, this stock will provide us with 12p of earnings per £1 invested in the stock, which is considerably higher than the return provided by many conventional investments. As stock investors, we should insist on a return of several percentage points above bonds and other investment instruments, given our **residual claim on assets**. Granted, it is unlikely that all the 12p in earnings will be distributed to us as shareholders, but it nevertheless provides a useful measure to implement as part of an investment thesis.

Price-to-Book Ratio

The book value of a business is usually determined from its breakup value, i.e. the dilution of its tangible assets if it went bankrupt or bust. The ratio of the current share price to its tangible book value per share is classed as the **price-to-book, or price-to-equity ratio**. This metric has more relevance in valuing companies that are asset-based, such as property trusts, as opposed to companies that have few tangible assets on their balance sheet. As with the P/E ratio, this metric should not be used as a sole measure and can differ widely between sectors and businesses. Nevertheless, it provides an important valuation metric to consider in a holistic appraisal. Be warned that the value of a company's assets can be difficult to determine, especially if the assets relate to intellectual property, brands, and technological applications for instance. Traditional businesses in manufacturing and construction are more easily valued given their use of plant and other equipment that are more easily quantified by accountants.

During stock market corrections and bear markets, it's not unusual to find businesses trading at less than their equity value (per share) on the balance sheet, potentially representing a solid bargain for investors with cash to burn. This feeds into the concept known as **margin of safety** that has been highlighted by legendary investors such as Benjamin Graham, Warren Buffett, Seth Klarman, Walter Schloss, Joel Greenblatt and Phil Town to name a few. Stocks that are trading at low P/E and P/B multiples usually outperform over the long-term, as prices tend to revert to their historical average, the so-called **reversion to the mean**.

To calculate the price to book ratio, we simply divide the current share price by the book value per share. For our recurring example, we first need to work out the book value per share. This information can be obtained from the company balance sheet, available on their website or your brokerage platform. For the sake of illustration, let's assume our example is as follows:

£5bn [assets] - £2.5bn [liabilities] = **£2.5bn** [equity]

Then, we divide the equity by the number of shares in issue to approximate the book value per share:

£2.5bn [equity] / 2bn [issued shares] = **£1.25** [book value per share]

Following this, we calculate the ratio of the current stock price, divided by the book value per share to get the P/B ratio:

100p [share price] / 125p [book value per share] = **0.8x**

In this case, our stock is trading at a 20% discount to its net asset value, or book value. As with the P/E ratio and many other metrics, this needs to be considered in the context of other businesses in the same sector, as well as broader market and historical averages. **There may be a fundamental reason why the stock is trading at such a discount**, but theoretically we are provided with a cushion of 20%. If the company were to be broken up now we would get back more than the price on a per-share basis.

Price-Earnings Growth Ratio (PEG)

The price-earnings growth (PEG) ratio adapts the P/E by adjusting for the earnings growth of a company. For our example company, assuming annual earnings growth of 15%, the PEG is calculated as follows:

P/E ratio: 100p [share price] / 12p [trailing EPS] = **8.3x**

PEG: 8.3 [P/E ratio] / 15% [earnings growth rate] = **0.6**

A PEG ratio of less than 1 represents an undervalued or desirable stock. We can also adjust the PEG ratio to account for the dividend yield of the stock, and this is of prime importance in our investing strategy:

Dividend-adjusted PEG: 8.3 [P/E ratio]/ (15 [earnings growth rate, %] + 6 [dividend yield, %]) = **0.4**

The inclusion of dividend income in the calculation reduces the ratio further. On this basis, our hypothetical stock is beginning to look like a bargain, and worthy of consideration in our portfolio.

Financial Health

Use of Debt

An appraisal of a company's financial health is an important component of the analysis. If the balance sheet is leveraged up with debt, this can sometimes be a bad thing, especially if interest rates go up over time. In general, a **debt-to-equity ratio** of less than 1 is ideal, but again this depends on the nature of the business and the sector it operates in. As with many others, this metric is often calculated for you on sites like Yahoo Finance and Morningstar. However, it's usually a good idea to screen the company webpages for the most up-to-date annual report or trading statement, to get reliable data. By dividing the total liabilities by the shareholder equity, we can calculate the debt-to-equity ratio. For our example this would be as follows:

£2.5bn [total liabilities] / £2.5bn [shareholder equity] = **1x**

Total liabilities are on par with shareholder equity but do not exceed total assets (£5bn), so in this case the leverage would be regarded as acceptable. If the company is using debt to fuel growth and expansion, and has a logical strategy to boot, this might be regarded as an effective use of capital and is likely to result in greater EPS and dividends over time. By contrast, if a company uses excess leverage to make ill-advised acquisitions, this could herald financial oblivion.

Profitability

Several ratios can be used to measure the profitability of a company for comparison with previous accounting periods or industry norms. **Operating margin** is net operating income divided by net sales or revenue and provides an insight into how much profit a company makes per dollar of revenue, after paying for the costs of production, such as materials and wages. **Net profit margin** evaluates the overall efficiency of management and is calculated by dividing net income by net revenue. This works similarly to operating margin but accounts for borrowing, investments and taxes. If a company is well run, with a long-term outlook, it will tend to generate higher profit margins by investing spare funds wisely, behaving economically with expenses, and operating in a tax-efficient manner. Lastly, **return on equity** is net income divided by stockholder's equity, and represents bottom line earnings as a percentage of the money that has been invested in the business. In simple terms, this ratio measures how effectively management is using the company's assets to create profits. To illustrate, a return on equity of ~15% would be considered average, whereas one below 10% would be regarded as poor.

All the information required to calculate these outcomes is publicly available (for instance on Morningstar, Yahoo Finance, Bloomberg and others) or can be easily obtained from financial reports and company statements online. These profitability ratios form an integral part of investment appraisal and should be wisely considered in your analysis.

Free Cash Flow

A central consideration when poring over a company's balance sheet is **free cash flow (FCF)**. In my opinion, this is one of the foremost financial considerations when appraising stocks and is often my first port of call when weighing up a business. Free cash flow equates to the funds a business generates after adjusting for capital expenditures (i.e., spending on equipment and infrastructure) and changes in working capital. It provides a useful indicator of the sustainability of future dividend payments and the ability to pay off debt, as well as highlighting financial elements that the income statement doesn't include. Information relating to cash flows can be found on the cash flow statement in the company financials pages or annual report. As with many metrics, FCF can be expressed on a per-share basis, as in this example:

Table 1. Free cash flow determination for John Smith Rivets plc

Cash flow statement	Amount in £m
Cash flow from operating activities	3,200
Interest expenses	50
Capital expenditures	20

From the above information, we can calculate FCF for this example company by adding interest back on to the cash generated from operating activities, and then subtracting capex. This gives us **£3.23 billion**, which when divided by the 2 billion shares in issue, equates to 161.5p per share. The share price divided by the per share FCF suggests a ratio of **1.6x**. A low price/FCF ratio such as this indicates that a company is undervalued and therefore likely to increase given a sufficient timeframe.

The statistics and calculations presented in this book are not exhaustive and this is intentional, **as we aren't training to be accountants or financial advisors**. Rather, we are using relatively simple math to build a picture of the state of a business in comparison with its peers. It is vitally important to look at debt, earnings over time, dividend growth, sustainability, and free cash flow. Don't just take my word for it – legendary investor and hedge fund manager Seth Klarman has stressed the usefulness of simple indicators and calculations when used with a long-term perspective in mind.

Management Effectiveness and Quality

Alongside the statistics detailed above, an appreciation of the effectiveness of management is critical if you are to make well- informed stock selections. This can be **more art than science**, involving a degree of qualitative thought. How well does management utilise the resources, or assets, of the company? What return is generated for shareholders from the resources at their disposal, such as shareholder equity, assets, and debt?

We looked at **return on equity** in the previous chapter as a measure of profitability, yet this also provides an insight into the effectiveness of management. Taken further, we can also determine **return on capital employed (ROCE)**, which accounts for all cash available to management, such as long-term debt facilities. This is calculated by dividing the earnings before interest and taxes (EBIT) by the capital employed. For our example business, this would be worked out as follows:

EBIT: £500,000,000

Capital employed: £5bn (total assets) − £1bn (current liabilities) = £4bn of capital employed

ROCE: £500,000,000/£4bn = 0.125 or **12.5%**

This example subtracts current liabilities (those falling due within one year) from the available capital. It demonstrates that for every £1 of capital employed by management, the company generates 12.5p of value for investors. A high ROCE suggests that a company is able to produce more earnings from each £1 of capital it employs. This can then be reinvested at a higher rate of return. In general, the ROCE should exceed prevailing interest rates to justify putting money into the business, and in our example, this is most certainly the case.

Insider Ownership

As a prospective shareholder, it's important to weigh up the intrinsic quality of the company management using the metrics explained in the previous chapters. In a more basic sense, we also **need to consider whether the company directors have some 'skin in the game'.** If none of them own a stake in the company, why should we take anything they say seriously? Are they working in line with the best interests of the company, and more importantly, **us as the owners?** Are their salaries excessive given the value they bring to the company?

It's possible to see who the largest shareholders of a business are by browsing through annual reports and investor relations pages. Usually, any entity or person holding more than 5% of a company's stock must be made public. Quite often, the largest stockholders will be institutions such as banks, pension and hedge funds, particularly for 'blue chip' companies. For smaller companies, the directors may be in the top five owners list, which is generally encouraging in that they have a stake in the business and should be working in line with investors' interests. If a director makes a purchase of shares in the company, it signals their confidence in the underlying business and its prospects. Conversely, if a director sells stock before financial results are released, this may raise eyebrows with regulatory authorities and could serve as a harbinger of bad news.

Margin of Safety and Economic Moat

When stocks are out of favour it's perfectly possible to come across bargains where a company is trading at less than its net asset value, or book value. It is also usually the case that these stocks comprise low earnings multiples and have inflated dividend yields. In the UK, Brexit-related uncertainty over the last two or three years has had a tremendous impact on these variables. Many companies are trading at attractive valuations and have nice dividend yields. They possess strong balance sheets, cash-generation potential, and are well-managed enterprises. Furthermore, many of these companies derive their earnings from overseas, in non-Sterling currencies. Amidst all this so-called 'uncertainty', the time seems right to buy discounted companies in the UK, to hold for the long term.

A great number of these stocks are trading at **way below their intrinsic value,** so in purchasing them you are provided with a **margin of safety**. In stock investing, we can never be 100% sure of a decision to buy a block of shares. By ensuring that a margin of safety exists, we can insulate ourselves somewhat against bad decisions resulting from not seeing the complete picture. Not only does this concept feed into the book value of a business, it also applies to the passive income or dividends that are thrown off. If a stock has a conservative payout ratio of between 30 – 50%, and has steadily growing earnings over time, we can be confident that the dividend will not be under threat and may in fact be robustly increased. As I've mentioned several times already, this is the real key to growing wealth for the future using shares.

Another central tenet of investing is the **economic moat** provided by certain companies. This is a function of brand identity or market dominance and represents a valuable consideration. Take Apple for example; arguably the most famous technology brand in the world, with the coveted iPhone serving as one of the most recognisable items in popular culture. It is *the* device to own and has been a cultural phenomenon. Every time a new iteration is released, customers flock to acquire it. These people might be more aptly referred to as fans instead of customers, as they will always be closely attached to the company and its products. This means that it is very difficult, if not impossible, for any new competitors to enter the scene and disrupt Apple's market share.

The economic moat can be applied to a great number of companies across a wide array of sectors. Coca-Cola is one of the most well-known and successful stocks in history, due to the uniqueness of its product and ubiquity throughout the world. Banks and large financial institutions, barring major crises, have a prominent and virtually unassailable place in society because of their provision of loans, mortgages, insurance, pensions and the like. Utilities like electricity and water, oil and gas, as well as property trusts all play an essential role and it is very difficult for others to get a foothold in the market, particularly when companies must comply with government regulations and the like.

Make no mistake, stock investing is harder these days than when Benjamin Graham was coming up with his formulas, as so many more players are in the market and there is abundant information available. **He also stated that his calculations are not gospel.** The essence of stock selection is in **weighing up the intrinsic value of what you're buying,**

and whether it is trading at a good price. Think about whether you would buy the entire business, if you could, fully aware of the considerations described here and chiefly, **how much passive income would the company generate for you?** Ask yourself whether any major threats to the cash flow exist.

PART III
Putting Things into Practice

Building a Portfolio from Scratch

Once you have decided to purchase your first stock, you will need to make a deal with your broker to add the shares to your portfolio. Initially, you should check to make sure that enough funds are in your brokerage account to finance a prospective trade. If you are based in the United Kingdom, I advise that you have at least £500 for each trade to minimise the impact of fees and taxes on your returns. If you can afford to invest more on a regular basis, that's great, but nonetheless I would recommend £500 as a bare minimum. Following this, you can make a deal for £500 of stock, inclusive of charges (commission, tax and so on). Usually you will get ~15 seconds to decide on a quote, but minute fluctuations such as this will not matter over the long-term.

Now that you've bought the stock you will receive a contract note as proof of purchase and can pretty much forget about it for a few days. However, I would advise that you **monitor the stock as if you are the owner of the business**. That is to say, you should take an interest in earnings updates, annual reports and statements. You must follow the journey of the business and monitor the cash flows that are likely to be returned to you. Consider the role of the board and directors - are they running the company well on your behalf? **This is what differentiates stock ownership from speculation!** Stocks are more than just lines on a screen to investors. Now that you own a position in a business, try not to obsess over minute fluctuations in the share price. Unless you intend to sell your holding in the next few months why should you care about short-term price movements? If you bought a car, farm, or house you wouldn't get it valued on a second-by-second basis, would you?

Diversification: The Only Free Lunch in Investing

Since you now have your first stock in your portfolio, how do you plan to expand and add further positions? I discussed earlier that you don't want to have all your eggs in one basket, but you also don't particularly want to mirror the generic results of the market. **If you are too concentrated in one sector you could get wiped out during a downturn, and it's highly unlikely that you will be able to predict the crash and get out in time.** Therefore, it is optimal to diversify across sectors, owning between 20 – 30 stocks, and follow the general principles above to enhance the likelihood of success. To help with this process, stock screeners can be extremely useful and do a lot of the work for you. Sources like Yahoo Finance and Morningstar can be invaluable in this regard.

The prudent passive income investor should diversify across the full gamut of sectors. These are as follows, with associated examples:

- Oil and Gas *Pipelines, Refining*
- Utilities *Water, Electricity*
- Consumer Staples *Food, Beverages*
- Consumer Discretionary *Video Games, Film, Music, Technology*
- Healthcare *Pharmaceuticals, Medical Supplies*
- Financials *Banking, Insurance, Mortgages, Pensions*

- Basic Materials *Mining, Lumber, Steel,*
- Property *Rental Homes, Hotels, Senior Housing, Commercial*

All these sectors should be represented in your portfolio to some degree, without any one position assuming too large a piece of the pie. Consider diversifying your portfolio by building a blue-chip 'backbone' or foundation – well-established businesses in your domestic market – and complement this with a select few smaller companies that have the capacity for accelerated expansion. **Don't forget that dividend payments are paramount and should be an essential feature of any addition to your portfolio.** Invest in businesses that you understand, i.e., you comprehend how they derive cash flows and generate growth.

I would strongly urge that you ignore broker news and views when selecting which stocks to add to your holdings. Perform your own research and make informed decisions without following the prevailing trends. This is where you will hold an advantage – by not being influenced or biased by the inconsistent noise and projections of the market. Within the space of a week, two separate equity analysts gave opposing views of a prominent UK retailer I was valuing. **Are you honestly telling me that the fundamental intrinsic worth of the business changed within the space of a week?** Barring some highly revelatory information, this is extremely unlikely and serves to illustrate the discord in the professional trading community. They can't win at their own game!

International Investing: It's a Big World Out There

Notwithstanding the Brexit-related uncertainty here in the UK, and the attractive opportunities this represents, it would be a shame to miss out on international stocks by restricting investments to our nation of residence. What's more, a **key part of diversification is by geography and locality, not solely by business sectors.** To ignore enticing opportunities around the world is incredibly foolish and leaves you vulnerable to geographical risk.

The beauty about dividend income is that it can be earned from companies all over the world, in non-domestic currencies. There are a huge number of successful businesses that comply with our investing ethos. It is crucial not to limit yourself to investing exclusively in domestic stocks. As I alluded to in the introduction, many pension funds simply invest every month in an index like the FTSE All-Share, regardless of price, instead of pursuing exciting opportunities overseas. Wherever you live, consider the investment opportunities that exist on an international level, and follow the same principles outlined in this book. What makes international investing so novel is the fact that **it provides a hedge against inflation.** If your domestic government is wildly irresponsible and inflates the currency, your international income should translate into greater amounts of your domestic currency.

Depending on who you ask, it is recommended that between 30 – 50% of your portfolio should be allocated to overseas stocks. You need to consider the tax implications of this, particularly with relation to withholding taxes. This can get complicated, and there are several treaties to negotiate, depending on where you live and where you own the stocks. These taxes can be mitigated somewhat by the dividend return, stock price increases and/or currency exchange benefits. However, there are also foreign exchange (FX) costs associated with transacting the stocks that will be levied on you by your broker. Therefore, a great deal of thought and care needs to be placed upon selecting the target market and stocks of interest to make things worthwhile.

I myself have benefitted from holding two specific US stocks during the Brexit uncertainty of the past three years. The dollar strengthened against Sterling and my overseas dividend income and stock value increased. Had it gone the other way, and the dollar weakened, it would have represented a **great opportunity to add to my positions at a more attractive price.** If this sounds confusing, there are a great number of investment products that can do the hard work for you, and I'll explain these in the next chapter.

One final consideration is that your broker may not have access to the markets that you are interested in investing in. This problem can be addressed by setting up a brokerage account with a company from inside the host nation. This will only really be worthwhile for individuals with substantial capital to transfer, but nevertheless should be a long-term goal for those of you seeking real wealth and prosperity. **Your fundamental vision should be to build assets all over the world, to diversify and pursue your dream life, unrestricted by the limitations of one particular nation or market.**

Passive Investing Strategies: Taking a Back Seat

Perhaps understandably, many readers will not have the willpower, patience, interest, or desire to select their own stocks and build their portfolios from scratch. This is fine, and there are a number of passive investing strategies and products that can be implemented to lower the burden on your time and level of commitment. Others may want to invest internationally for diversification but don't necessarily want the headaches of dealing with FX transaction costs and the complexities of unfamiliar markets. To this end, similar products can be utilised to take away the fuss and let you get on with life.

One method is to use index investing strategies, in which you buy into a fund that is balanced to represent, or track, a stock market index such as the FTSE 100 or S&P 500. These funds benefit from low expense ratios (the amount you have to pay each year to own the fund) and have tended to outperform mutual funds (funds that are actively managed by a fund manager). Mutual funds have higher expense ratios due to this active management, which **eats into returns from the outset**. Many of these funds underperform their benchmark indices over the long term and do not warrant the fees that investors end up paying. In time, these percentage point charges equate to huge amounts of profit that **don't end up in your pocket**. Although I recognise that there are some fantastic fund managers out there, I do not recommend mutual funds and they are not a product I have ever invested in.

My own personal strategy, given my focus on income and yield, would be to consider **dividend-focused exchange-traded funds**

(ETFs). These instruments have been increasingly used for speculative purposes by traders, but they can be fantastic ways to gain exposure to international stocks, as well as for portfolio diversification. An ETF is a passive investment instrument that trades on an exchange like a stock, but what it really represents is **a basket of stocks**.

Each ETF has its own objectives and remit. There are some that track the FTSE 100 like an index fund and have similar expense ratios to boot (around 0.2%). Remember however that by holding the index these funds will own stocks that don't pay dividends, which lies counter to our investment goals. Correspondingly, the yield on these ETFs can be rather low. For instance, the S&P 500 currently yields around 2%, which is pretty much the interest rate offered by savings accounts at banks. After fees and taxes are paid, not to mention inflation, there is very little if any income left over.

Alternatively, there are other ETFs that sit more in line with our yield-hunting objectives. Some examples of these products are the Vanguard FTSE All-World High Dividend ETF, the iShares International Select Dividend ETF, the iShares Asia-Pacific Dividend ETF, and the iShares Emerging Markets Dividend ETF. Although these products tend to have higher expense ratios than run of the mill index ETFs, they usually have higher yields. Most dividend ETFs also pay out income on a quarterly basis and increase these payments over time.

As a point of focus, the iShares Asia-Pacific Dividend ETF presently yields around 6% and comprises 30 businesses with leading dividend yields in Singapore, Australia, and New Zealand to name a few. This ETF provides international diversification in an area of attractive economic growth, owning robust businesses in fundamental sectors to society, and throws off growing dividend income every quarter. Dividend ETFs such as this own a basket of stocks, collect all dividend income from their holdings, keep the cash in an account, and then pay out distributions to their investors at management's discretion. They also have the choice, like we do as income investors, to reinvest the income into their underlying holdings.

It is crucial to consider exactly what is in the ETF, as the basket is only as good as what is in it, as well as the **price of said basket.** The ETF holdings can be found on the product website alongside the management costs and investment prospectus. As always, if you decide to add such a product to your portfolio **make use of the income by compounding it into other income-producing assets.**

Hopefully you can see how ETFs represent a powerful means of diversifying your assets across regions and markets whilst pursuing income. What I would avoid is the flashy, niche ETFs that focus on a specific sector or new fad, such as cryptocurrency or technology, as many of these are subject to major gyrations in price and do not produce robust cash flows to enable compounding to take place.

A Word on Mutual Funds

If your broker is anything like mine, periodically you will be sent literature advertising managed funds, either with them or other reputable providers. So-called mutual funds, in this sense, are actively managed entities where the investor pays someone with more knowledge, time, skill and resources to invest their money for them. **This service isn't free** of course; the fund will take an ongoing charge that could be around 100 basis points (1%). This purportedly pays for the running costs of the fund, including marketing and distribution. There may also be entry and exit charges when you buy in or sell out of the fund, and these charges could be in the region of around 2.5%. The management fee is taken even if the fund underperforms its benchmark indices (i.e., the FTSE 100 or S&P500), and this is something of a concern.

Earlier, we examined the importance of one percentage point with respect to investment returns, and how we need to maximise yield whilst controlling for risk. I recognise that there are some superb fund managers that can accomplish tremendous things but the data show that mutual funds underperform the market over the long term. In paying a fund manager, **you take all the risk by giving them your capital**, and they could lose most of it and still take their cut. Mutual funds also have to invest in stocks with a large amount of liquidity on the market to make it cost effective and worthwhile for them. They have to buy as the market grows and more people pour cash into the fund, fuelling the hype. They then have to sell cheaply when investors flee, exacerbating the collapse. In chasing their short-term goals, which involve performing in line with their benchmarks, many fund managers don't have your long-term objectives in focus.

The bottom line is this: if you're not prepared to learn about the specifics of passive income investing yourself, choose a strategy that simplifies matters and, most importantly, **minimises the costs as much as possible.** In this regard, the use of passive strategies with a focus on income, such as dividend ETFs (domestic and international) as mentioned in the previous chapter, could represent the best way forward.

Mortgage or REIT?

Lots of people I encounter in day-to-day life express a desire to own a home, a wish that sounds perfectly acceptable when taken at face value. Home ownership has long been viewed as a marker of adulthood and success. What this means **in real terms** however is that they intend to put a deposit down on a property of around £30,000, borrow the remaining £200,000, and tie themselves into a contract for 30 years; based on current conventions and average house price assumptions in the UK. The perceived wisdom of taking on a mortgage for this length of time, as opposed to buying a home outright eventually, has irritated me for quite a while and hopefully this chapter will illustrate why.

Firstly, by taking on a mortgage **the bank owns the home, not you.** Many people believe that they are building equity in a property by making their monthly payments, but in reality they are paying off interest for the first ~15 years of the mortgage. If a mortgage is used to fund a buy-to-let, the owner must contend with an overvalued housing market, tax implications, and myriad rules and regulations. The dream of owning a home has historically been cultivated by banks and financial institutions because it makes them money. If your objective is to buy property for investment, I would argue that **it is much better to purchase a real estate investment trust, or REIT, and let the landlord do the work for you.**

A REIT is basically a property trust that owns real estate in a specific sector, for instance residential buildings, offices, hotels, warehouses, shops, self-storage, retirement facilities and so forth. The property portfolio is managed on shareholders' behalf and the rent collected from tenants each month. A so-called 'registered REIT' will distribute around 90% of this income to shareholders of the REIT. This is decreed by law - they are **literally compelled to pay you as the investor!** Therefore, I would propose that it is far better to gain exposure to the property market using REITs, build your assets and cash flows, let the landlord deal with the headaches of property management, while you sit back and **collect quarterly passive income.** Many REITs in the UK and elsewhere are trading at discounts to book value and offer high dividend yields (~6 – 9%) with attractive dividend growth rates. If the property market goes up, the net asset value of the REIT will also rise, allowing you to participate in the capital appreciation of the portfolio if you sell the stock.

In this scenario, the **impact of opportunity cost is clear.** On the one hand, you can spend 30 years of your life to pay two or three times more than a house is worth, at an interest rate that is subject to change on the whims of a central bank. Alternatively, you may instead plough your spare income into REIT portfolios around the world and **collect truly passive income**, then buy your dream house for cash one day when you are financially abundant.

To illustrate this concept, the present Bank of England base interest rate is 0.75%. A prominent high street building society in the UK has a base mortgage rate of 2.75%, and they assert that this will never be more than 2% above the Bank of England rate. Their standard mortgage rate at present is 4.24%. Assuming you get a mortgage on a house of average price (£230,000) with a 10% deposit (£23,000), this leaves

£207,000 to pay, or around £1,017 per month for 30 years. The amount of interest you would pay over those 30 years would amount to £159,106, or ~45% of the property value. Therefore, the house would need to increase in value by ~45% **to justify the cost of locking ourselves in to the mortgage.** Of course, this assumes that interest rates remain the same (hopefully they don't go up!) and the housing market doesn't fall through the floor like it did in 2008.

Conversely, we could instead take the £23,000 deposit and invest it in a suitable REIT portfolio, diversified by sector and geography, for an example yield of around 7%. In a tax-sheltered account, over the same amount of time with income reinvestment, the deposit would grow in excess of £500,000 and be throwing off ~£35,000 in annual income, based on dividend growth of 4% per year. If you paid in £10,000 per year on top of this income reinvestment, the principal will swell to around £2.6 million after 30 years, paying out ~£183,000 each year in dividends. **This is life-changing money.** Equally as important is the fact that in doing this, you avoid a costly liability over the period and maintain a significant degree of freedom and independence.

When to Sell

One of the most difficult decisions to make in investing is when to get out of a position. Make no mistake, **the ideal stock is the one you can buy and forget**, that continues to build earnings and dividends over time. However, this doesn't always hold true, even if our calculations and assumptions are sound. It should also be noted that very few, if any, businesses endure in perpetuity. To my mind, there are several scenarios in which a sale should be considered:

- If the P/E ratio exceeds 45 the stock could be regarded as significantly overvalued and it might be best to take the profits and reinvest in a more attractive proposition.

- If the initial assumptions that were made about the business no longer apply with regards to earnings growth, dividend yield, return on capital and so forth. It is entirely possible that a mistake could have been made when appraising the company, and it would be far better to rectify this in the short-term to reinvest in a better opportunity elsewhere.

- A cut in the dividend, or worse yet an abolition of it, violates the passive income assumptions that are central to the investment strategy. A dividend growth rate that begins to stagnate may also be a justifiable reason to sell and pursue other opportunities.

- You may be forced to sell the stock in the event of an acquisition by another company, a cash-for-stock merger, or other action taken by the board that results in the sale of your shareholdings.

- In a similar vein to the previous point, if a company issues new shares of stock this will dilute the earnings allocated to the pre-existing shares. It is probable that the dividend will be cut or abolished entirely prior to this point. This scenario differs from a stock split, where shares increase to a particular value and are then split to enhance liquidity in the market. Your ownership stake doesn't change in this situation, so there is little to fear.

- Lastly, there may be a scenario when you need the money for whatever reason. Whilst this should be avoided under normal circumstances, since you may be forced to sell at a less than desirable price; sometimes life throws unpredictable curveballs that we simply cannot avoid. **This is a worst-case scenario however.**

Whatever your rationale for selling, the consideration of tax implications is paramount. Remember that passive income from dividends in a tax-liable account are subject to a lower rate of tax than capital gains and salaried income, depending on your country of residence. Provided the underlying assumptions and rationale are sound from the outset, you won't be required to sell your holdings except in rare circumstances.

Evaluating Performance and Success

As with most other worthwhile fields, it is incredibly important to document successes and failures. In doing this, you can better understand the choices that led to these events and refine your strategy over time. The best way to document this is to **make notes of every transaction you carry out, and the underlying rationale for each one.** A journal or ledger book is ideal for this purpose, either hard copy or online, and this can be used to track investment performance. Alongside your broker reports, usually provided each quarter, you can complement these methods by compiling your own spreadsheet to support this analysis. Below I have included **two case studies** to illustrate how I evaluate the performance of my own shareholdings.

Case Study 1: Under Construction

In September of 2016 I was looking to buy shares in a UK construction company, given the persistent housing shortage in the country and overvalued nature of the market. I bought 120 shares in a blue-chip housebuilder at a price of 470p each, for a total transaction cost (less fees) of £564. My dividend eligibility in 2016 was 24.7p per share; this increased to 41.7p in 2017, 43.8p in 2018, with an interim payment of 9.6p due in May 2019. For 2017 and 2018 (i.e. the two full and complete years that I have owned the stock) the **yield on cost was 8.9% and 9.3%**, respectively.

This scenario indicates that as of May this year, I will have received £143.76 in dividends, a **return of 25.5% in dividends alone.** This money has been redeployed into other opportunities along the way and continues to compound. When considering capital appreciation, the stock currently trades at a price of 615.20p, meaning that my shareholding is now worth £738.24. The **total return**, if I were to sell my position right now, is therefore £738.24 + £143.76 = **£882** / £564 − 1 * 100 = **56.4%.** As I alluded to in Part II, dividends have accounted for around half of the total return for this specific holding.

Since my transaction and commencement of ownership, earnings and operating margins have increased each year. Moreover, ROCE has hovered between 20 − 30%, and this is very satisfactory. Given the prevailing housing environment in the UK, it seems reasonable to expect that earnings and dividend growth will continue for some time to come. I will be monitoring the business to ensure that it maintains cash and value generation, and only look to sell when my central tenets are violated.

Case Study 2: As Good as Gold

To complement the blue-chip example above, I also invested in a smaller enterprise − a gold mining company trading on the UK exchange, but based predominantly in Eastern Europe. Gold is an important 'safe haven' asset during recessionary periods and economic turmoil. My initial rationale was that I wanted a stock that was 'younger' and thus having more attractive growth opportunities, but also had a strong commitment to dividend payments. As it happens, this stock was trading at a low P/E multiple and a 35% discount to its net asset value. More importantly, it offered a ~7% dividend yield; with management holding significant ownership in the company and looking to expand its asset base. I purchased 263 shares at 147.50p each in April 2018, for a total transaction cost (less fees) of £387.92. I had programmed in a **margin of safety** and, given the company's commitment to pay out 20% of net cash flow from operating activities, I was happy to wait and see. The dividend commitment seemed reasonable, especially given the capital-intensive nature of mining per se.

Since the purchase I have received £43.18 in dividends, **a return of 11.1% in one year**. The shares currently trade at 165.80p each, so therefore my total return is £436.05 + £43.18 = **£479.23** / £387.92 – 1 * 100 = **23.5%**. This is very satisfactory after holding the stock for 12 months and once again, the dividend return is a huge component, constituting **just under half of the total return**. This is in line with the broader statistics reported in Part II. Small-cap companies offer nice growth opportunities such as this as they garner less attention from big Wall Street analysts and can disappear under the radar.

Closing Thoughts

I hope I've presented a thorough and convincing rationale for passive income investing using dividend-paying stocks and inspired you to go ahead and research the area yourselves. By applying the principles here and diligently building a dividend stock portfolio, alongside other income-producing assets, maybe one day you can achieve financial independence and prosperity.

Stock investing can be incredibly challenging but also extremely rewarding. In participating and doing well, you will never again have to worry about working to live, and can enjoy the full breadth of life's experiences. Support your family and those close to you, donate to charities of your choice, travel the world, or just have fun and bask in your own success. That is the power of freedom and I have every faith in your ability to attain it.

I wish you the very best with your financial and career objectives. Good luck!

Reading List: Taking Things Further

The following list comprises several legendary and foundational texts that are indispensable for the novice with an interest in investing, finance, capitalism, and economics:

The Essays of Warren Buffett: Lessons for Corporate America by Lawrence A. Cunningham

Principles by Ray Dalio

Common Stocks and Uncommon Profits by Philip A. Fisher

Capitalism and Freedom by Milton Friedman

The Motley Fool's Million Dollar Portfolio by David and Tom Gardner

The Intelligent Investor by Benjamin Graham

Security Analysis by Benjamin Graham and David Dodd

The Little Book That Still Beats the Market by Joel Greenblatt

The Road to Serfdom by Friedrich Hayek

Buffett: The Making of an American Capitalist by Roger Lowenstein

Beating the Street by Peter Lynch

Conscious Capitalism by John Mackey and Rajendra Sisodia

Bull Moves in Bear Markets by Peter Schiff

The Wealth of Nations by Adam Smith

Misbehaving: The Making of Behavioural Economics by Richard H. Thaler

About the Publisher

Founded in 2018, Rising Tide Press is a small independent publisher of selected fiction, self-help, finance and education titles.